Insightful and heartfelt! Every broken person needs to read this message of triumph. Sharllette's message of hope is a gift to the world.

—E.C. Maltbia,
Founder and Senior Pastor of True Holiness Saints Center

Single
and
Pregnant

Single
and
Pregnant
A New Beginning

Sharllette Berry

Single and Pregnant?

Copyright © 2020 by Sharllette Berry. All rights reserved.

No part of this publication may be reproduced, stored in a retrieval system or transmitted in any way by any means, electronic, mechanical, photocopy, recording or otherwise without the prior permission of the author except as provided by USA copyright law.

Scripture quotations marked (amp) are taken from the *Amplified Bible*, Copyright

© 1954, 1958, 1962, 1964, 1965, 1987 by The Lockman Foundation. Used by permission.

Scripture quotations marked (nkjv) are taken from the *New King James Version*®. Copyright © 1982 by Thomas Nelson, Inc. Used by permission. All rights reserved.

Scripture quotations marked (nlt) are taken from the *Holy Bible, New Living Translation*, copyright © 1996. Used by permission of Tyndale House Publishers, Inc., Wheaton, Illinois 60189. All rights reserved.

This book is designed to provide accurate and authoritative information with regard to the subject matter covered. This information is given with the understanding that neither the author is engaged in rendering legal, professional advice. Since the details of your situation are fact dependent, you should additionally seek the services of a competent professional.

Author photo courtesy of Jai Brands Photography

Published in the United States of America ISBN: 978-1-7362785-0-5

Religion: Christian Life: Women's Issues

Dedication

To the Almighty God my Father:
I thank you for hearing my cry
To you belongs all the glory.

To my parents:
Delbert and Rochelle Berry,
and Linda Price

To my daughter and darling angel:
Jaiden Elise Andrews-Berry

To every pregnant woman who has
fears about the future,
this is for you.

Acknowledgments

To Pastor E. C. and First Lady Natasha Maltbia, for staying by my side and not letting me get away.

To Miyake Lee, my spiritually knitted sister and best friend, thank you for just being you.

Table of Contents

Acknowledgments viii

Foreword xi

Introduction: It's Real 1

Emotions and Shock 5

Fears Calmed 11

The Word 15

Your Relationship 21

The Enemy's Lies 32

Making the Transition 42

Promotion 53

It's All about Seeds 58

Manifested Victory 66

Living the Promise 71

Foreword

Most precious daughter of God,

I am writing to you as a sister. A sister who is excited for you and wants you to know that your life is about to change, to never be the same again! "Well, of course," I hear you saying. "It doesn't take a genius to know that!" You are certainly correct! With your transforming figure, anyone with eyes is sure to know that your life is changing. However, the change that I am writing of is one that has little to do with your figure but all to do with a transformation within. My friend, never before has there been a book designed with your unique destiny in mind, the destiny of a soon to be, single mother. (And yes, God does have a great destiny for you!) Never before has there been more keen an insight into your specific situation than right here, right now, with this book. This message will certainly change your perspective concerning your pregnancy and that of your unborn child, but more importantly, it will be an anchor for your soul as you face the harsh winds of uncertainty and the heavy waves of guilt and condemnation. And, my friend, there is no better woman to remind you of God's love and provision for you during this time than Sharllette Berry. Though her name and face may be unfamiliar to you now, as you allow her words of wisdom and faith into your heart and mind, you will soon come to know the anointing on her life and trust it as none other than God's. I have personally been a recipient of the Father's love and encouragement through her life as she is my closest friend and the sister that God saw so clearly that I needed.

You may read her story and find that the circumstances that surrounded her pregnancy are totally different than your own. Or you may find that they are so similar until you just know she had to be hiding in your closet before writing this. The truth is, no matter the circumstance, God had you in mind. How do I know that without knowing you? The reason is simple, my sister. God knows that the enemy of your soul uses the same tactics and strategies against us all no matter the circumstances. He attacks you with guilt. He sets traps for you then brings condemnation when you get stuck! He brings thoughts in your mind, telling you how God "feels about you." He even tells you that you've just messed up too bad this time, that you should just quit. Sound familiar? Well, God knew that you would need a weapon to counter these attacks. He knew you needed to know the truth. He knew you needed to know that someone else had been through it. And no, it wasn't easy. But with God's help and love, she overcame, is living out her destiny with peace and joy, and expects with great hope for even greater things to come.

So, my sister, expect to meet God in these writings. Expect healing. Expect wisdom. And most of all, expect hope for all that is to come for you and your soon-coming baby!

—A living witness, Miyake A. Lee

Introduction: It's Real

You're pregnant for real this time. You can hardly believe the test results, but it's true: you're pregnant. Reality hits. One minute you are so numb that you are speechless. The next minute, you are on an emotional roller coaster. You may ask yourself, *What will they think? How will I ever make it? Will he be there?* These are just a few emotions that may be going through your head right now, but don't worry. Your help and answers have already been provided by God.

On the other hand, you may feel tremendous joy and excitement coupled with feelings of great expectations. Regardless of whether you are happy or sad about your pregnancy, this is no surprise to God. It may have surprised you, or maybe you even planned it. This may shock your family and friends, but you haven't shocked God. Despite your present situation and inability to predict the future, God remains sovereign.

How does she know that? you may wonder. Well, I have had firsthand experience. I was twenty and had just gotten out of a four-year relationship with my high school sweetheart. Honestly, I was on the rebound. I was heartbroken. He and I had grown apart, but it was still very painful to let go. I was trying to get on the path to know Jesus better, and he was doing just the opposite. I realized that it wasn't going to work, so to my disappointment, the relationship ended.

Now, I was free. Though I had always been faithful to him, I felt it was time to see what the world had to offer. In reality, it was the worst time to explore. I was in no shape to make a clear judgment about a mate because of the broken state I was in. Of course, this was not clear to me at the time, so I proceeded to find a companion (not for sex, but for friendship) to help medicate the pain. That's when I met him, the man who would soon be the father of my child.

I was looking at some CDs in a music store when he casually approached. He had smooth, gentleman-like conversation. So, of course, I obliged his offer to exchange numbers. Soon, one thing led to another, and there I was, pregnant with not even an official girlfriend title to show for it. My family barely knew him. They were still trying to get over the loss of their "son-in-law" that they had known throughout my high school years. The news of my pregnancy shocked my family, friends, and the church. Though I was only twenty years old, I acknowledged God's calling on my life at age nine- teen. I served my church as a ministerial staff member and leader for my church's college ministry at the University of Central Arkansas. I was an active praise team member in the music department. Oh, the shame and condemnation I felt seemed to be unbearable at times! I had gotten myself in a mess, and I didn't know if God could get me out. For me, abortion was not an option. I'd always loved babies, so I just decided I must find a way to deal with it. After overcoming many trials, I know that God yet reigns on the throne. This book contains my experiences and my testimony of how God brought me through. I hope my story encourages you by stirring your faith. God will make you more than an overcomer as well.

Emotions and Shock

Who knew it was possible to have so many feelings at once? True, I never imagined myself with a child and no husband, but I always wanted kids. Thoughts of excitement entered my mind when I imagined how my child might look. Would it be a girl or a boy? Hair or no hair? One second later, those thoughts were trampled to death with the fear of what my family would think of me.

If you recently discovered you are pregnant, I am sure these thoughts are very familiar to you. *What will my next step be? What kind of man will the father be to the baby? What if he leaves me?*

It didn't take very long for most of my questions to get answered. When you tell one person that you are pregnant, even if you swear that person to secrecy, the news is still sure to travel. Don't get upset about this. Circumstances like this will never stay silent for very long. I told a few friends, and close friends might I add, and the cat was still let out of the bag.

It was hard. Before long, it seemed the entire city knew. Some people acted with love and support, and others reacted with judgment. You may find the same to be true. If so, remember not to get upset. There are more important things to put your attention on. The shock of all of it will eventually settle, so refuse to be discouraged.

Pastoral Support

My pastor, E. C. Maltbia, knew just how judgmental and harsh people could be. I believe that's why he was one of my biggest supporters throughout my pregnancy. Though he never condoned my behavior, he never condemned me. He was always there to offer any support or encouragement when needed.

Pastor Maltbia was actually the first person Jason and I told.

It was late one winter night. Jason and I sat in complete shock when we looked at the positive result on the pregnancy test. My first thought was to pack my bags and move to another city. I already knew that I didn't want to face the ridicule or any other hardship that would come.

Jason wasn't thinking with any more sense than I was. I said to him, "Look, I know it is very late now, but I have to go tell my pastor." We then drove to my pastor's house at 2:00 a.m.

Pastor greeted us at the door and welcomed us inside. We sat down in his living room, and he asked us what was on our minds. We shared the news with him and told him about our decision to move out of the city. Then Pastor Maltbia wisely responded: "Don't make a permanent decision based on a temporary situation." Almost instantly, I realized how crazy my thinking was. I was making a quick decision while I was in panic mode. After all, I had just taken the pregnancy test hours earlier. I realized it probably wouldn't be easy, but I would have to face my fears of what people would think of me.

Allow my pastor's words of wisdom to serve as encouragement for you. Never make a permanent decision on a temporary situation. The shock of your pregnancy will only be for a short season. In time, people will adapt and move on with life. Do not allow this season to keep you burdened. The shock of it will be over soon.

I am so thankful for my pastor and his wife. If I were not under his guidance, I believe I would still be struggling right now. If you are already a Christian, let this serve as a reminder concerning the importance of being under the guidance and covering of a pastor that loves and supports you. It will help to keep you grounded in the emotional and vulnerable times.

If you have not developed a personal relationship with Jesus, or you need to recommit your life, please allow me this moment to introduce or reintroduce you to him. Jesus is the Son of God. According to John 14:6 (nkjv), He is the way, the truth, and the life. If you want to know your purpose in life, your very reason for being, you must go to your Creator, God. He has a purpose for your child as well. The only way to God, as stated in the Bible, is through Jesus.

The purpose for living and the purpose of your child can only be found in God. You can learn more about God at your church. So again, I cannot stress enough the importance of being in a good church home where biblical principles are being taught and the love of God is shown through the people.

Having a personal relationship with Jesus is where it all begins. Your life and the purpose of your child will not be fulfilled without a relationship with Jesus Christ. By the time you complete this book, you will see how the Lord will restore your life, heal your pain, and bless you with an abundant life, even as a single parent. This will come about only through a personal relationship with him.

Pray this prayer with me:

> Father, I come to you today as a sinner. I acknowledge Jesus Christ as your resurrected Son. I believe that he came and died on the cross for my sins.

> I acknowledge my faults to you, and I believe you are faithful to forgive me. I ask you to come into my heart and dwell there. Today, I believe you have given me a fresh start. Father, I ask you to lead me to a church home where I will be taught your word and my spirit will be fed. I thank you in advance for your guidance. Thank you for your mercy, forgiveness, and love. In Jesus' name, amen.

If you prayed and believed that prayer, no matter what happens, you have made your first step toward victory. If you do not have a church home, continue to pray for the Lord to guide you to the church he would have you to be in. Join, and stay close to the fire. Keeping people around who give their love and support is vital to your peace and joy in this season. Rejoice! You have a heavenly Father who loves you and has an awesome plan for your life and the life of your baby.

Fears Calmed

I would like to mention several things about fear. (1) Fear is paralyzing. (2) It is torment. (3) It is not from God and (4) is an open door for the devil to attack your mind. Fear must be overcome with faith in God's word. The Bible states in 2 Timothy 1:7 (nkjv), "For God has not given us a spirit of fear, but of power and of love, and of a sound mind." God gives us several tools to use. (1) God gives us power to overcome struggles, (2) the ability to love those who hurt us, and (3) peace for our minds.

Looking back, I remember how much I worried about my future. I worried about whether or not I would be a good parent. I worried about the type of relationship I would have with my child. I just worried, worried, and worried. Sound familiar?

Learn to take these concerns to God in prayer. I had to quickly learn that talking to God about how he needed to fix all my problems wasn't very effective in getting him to act on my behalf. I couldn't just wallow in my world of uncertainties. I also learned my prayers would not be productive if all I did was complain to God about what I didn't know about my future. I had to take another approach, the approach of faith—the prayer that pleases God.

This is a prayer based on his word, your faith, and thankfulness. Faith simply believes, regardless of the circumstances, that God *will* perform his word. What is his word? It is found throughout the scriptures. As a matter of fact, it *is* the scriptures. It is his word regarding provision, protection, and blessing. It is his power, his peace, and his joy given to all who will seek after and live for him. Even today, it is available to you. All it takes is your faith. Live by the word. Obey God's principles. He will not fail you!

Here is an example of how to pray with faith in God's word. When you truly believe God to perform his word, you thank him even before you see the manifestation.

Prayer of Faith

Father, I thank you that all things are in your control. Though I may not know right now what my tomorrow holds, I am putting my trust in you because my times are in your hands. Your word declares that I should not worry about anything, but pray about everything. You are my peace, and you keep those in perfect peace who keep their minds on you. I thank you for being my present help. You love me and will never fail me. Thank you, Father. In your son, Jesus' name, amen.

Scriptures

> But as for me, I trust in You, O Lord; I say, "You are my God." My times are in Your hand.
>
> Psalms 31:14-15a (nkjv)

Don't worry about anything, instead, pray about everything. Tell God what you need, and thank him for all he has done.

                                        Philippians 4:6 (nlt)

You will keep him in perfect peace whose mind is stayed on You, because he trusts in You.

                                        Isaiah 26:3 (nkjv)

God is our refuge and strength, a very present help in trouble.

                                        Psalms 46:1 (nkjv)

For God so loved the world, that He gave His only begotten Son, that whoever believes in Him should not perish but have everlasting life.

                                        John 3:16 (nkjv)

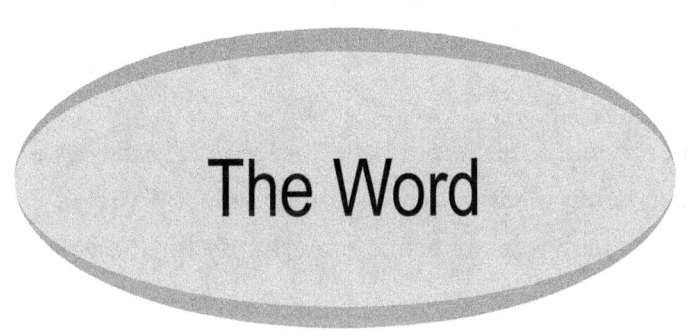

The Word

During my pregnancy, I was desperate, very desperate. I needed to know if his Word was true. I had heard so many people testify of God's ability to turn a situation around. Now, I was in a position in which I needed God to work for me. Everything around me didn't look good. My dreams for finishing college and having a prosperous life seemed as though they were going down the drain. If there was ever a time that I needed the word to work for me, it was now.

I began to read my Bible more. Though I had been a Christian for many years, I had not learned how to stand on the word. I desperately needed the scripture that states in Nehemiah 8:10 (nkjv), "The joy of the Lord is my strength," to be real to me and not just words in a book. I needed to have "peace that surpasses understanding" as stated in Philippians 4:7 (nkjv). My pregnancy was my prime opportunity for the word to become real.

Work the Word

Every time I had a negative or a depressing thought come to my mind, I would read a scripture. I would meditate on that scripture to keep my mind from dwelling on negative things. It was the only way for me to maintain my smile, and that smile would be from the joy that I had within. I began to see how meditating and believing the truths in God's word brought about a change in my thinking. My outlook on life began to change from depressed to hopeful as the scriptures were imbedded into my heart.

I had plenty of opportunities to take my mind off of God's word and place it on the uncertainties of life. It seemed as if each day some disappointment awaited me. But, regardless, I was desperate. I hated being depressed. If God's word was the way to a better day, I was taking it. I began to have faith that God would somehow fix my mess. I knew when God brought me out, I would have to give him all the glory for it, because I could naturally see no way out.

Even if you can't see how you will make it through this season in life, take your first step of faith by meditating on God's word. This can be a very fearful sea- son when considering the uncertainties of how your relationships will work out and how your financial responsibilities will change. But, it doesn't have to be. When you understand and have faith that God has already worked your future out, you can rest and have peace during your pregnancy. God will guide your steps to provision if you allow him. Here are some scriptures you can meditate on to help maintain your peace and stir your faith in this season.

Prayer of Faith

Father, I thank you for the truth of your word. Help me to give you all of my worries and concerns. Help me to put my trust in you that I may be in perfect peace. I thank you, even though I may not know where all of my provision is coming from, I know you will provide. I believe by faith that you have already made a way. Thank you for your love. In Jesus' name, amen.

Scriptures

> So, I tell you, don't worry about everyday life—whether you have enough food, drink, and clothes. Doesn't life consist of more than food and clothing? Look at the birds. They don't need to plant or harvest or put food in barns because your heavenly Father feeds them. And you are far more valuable to him than they are. Can all your worries add a single moment to your life? Of course not. And why worry about your clothes? Look at the lilies and how they grow. They don't work or make their clothing, yet Solomon in all his glory was not dressed as beautifully as they are. And if God cares so wonderfully for flowers that are here to- day and gone tomorrow, won't he more surely care for you? You have so little faith! So

don't worry about having enough food or drink or clothing. Why be like the pagans who are so deeply concerned about these things? Your heavenly Father already knows all your needs, and he will give you all you need from day to day if you live for him and make the Kingdom of God your primary concern.

Matthew 6:25-33 (nlt)

You will keep him in perfect peace, whose mind is stayed on You, because he trusts in You.

Isaiah 26:3 (nkjv)

And this same God who takes care of me will supply all your needs from his glorious riches, which have been given to us in Christ Jesus.

Philippians 4:19 (nlt)

By faith these people overthrew kingdoms, ruled with justice, and received what God had promised them. They shut the mouths of lions, quenched the flames of fire, and escaped death by the edge of the sword. Their weakness was turned to strength. They became strong in battle and put whole armies to flight.

Hebrews 11:33-34 (nlt)

Your Relationship

Maybe you were in a relationship with someone you really cared about, and you didn't want him to leave you. Maybe you thought that having his child was the answer. To you, my dear heart, I must say true love must come from truth. Let me clarify. If the man you are with does not recognize your worth as a woman, having a child will not cause him to see you in a different light.

A woman should never rely on anyone to make her feel loved. A woman is a blessing to her God-given mate when she is emotionally whole. Having a child to keep a mate describes a woman who is emotionally broken, operating in manipulation and desperately needing to know the love of God. If this is you, most likely you have experienced a lot of hurt in your life.

This is not the end of your story. Your future does not have to be determined by the pain of your past. Begin acknowledging your true intent of becoming pregnant to God. God already knew about the brokenness in your heart. Acknowledging your true intent will allow you to make the first step in becoming emotionally whole. God is more than able to make you complete without a man that never meant you well in the first place. God knows about all the hurt and pain you have experienced in your past.

Begin today with your truth confession, and wit- ness how God will put all your broken pieces back together again.

Prayer of Faith

Father, I am acknowledging that I am in need of your love. Allow me to experience your love like never before. Make me whole and complete. Heal all the pain of my past and help me to look forward to my future. No one can love me like you do. I thank you for the new thing you are doing in my life. In Jesus' name, amen.

Scriptures

> The Lord is close to the brokenhearted; he rescues those who are crushed in spirit.
>
> Psalm 38:18 (nlt)

> Behold, I will do a new thing, now it shall spring forth; Shall you not know it? I will even make a road in the wilderness and rivers in the desert.
>
> Isaiah 43:19 (nkjv)

What You Always Wanted

Maybe this category will better suit your situation. Feelings of joy overcame you when you discovered you were pregnant. You are in a seemingly great relation- ship with your boyfriend. You have always been certain that you wanted him to be the father of your children, and now, your dream can finally be made reality.

If you are certain your mate is God's choice for your life, then seek counseling from your pastor. With prayer and your pastor's guidance, the two of you can begin the journey of having a fulfilled life and destiny through God's design for marriage. There have been many God-ordained marriages (marriages that are in God's will) that have been successful, even though the sequence of events didn't mimic first love, next marriage, and then baby in the baby carriage.

However, if you are not certain this is God's choice mate for you, marriage is definitely not the road to take, no matter how much pressure you receive from friends or family. Marriage is a God-ordained institution and should not be used as a cover up or a quick fix for an unplanned pregnancy. This type of marriage promises to have many hard days. Before taking such a life-changing step, be certain that your mate is God's will for your life.

Prayer of Faith

Today, Father, I seek your direction. I trust you will lead me and guide me every step of the way. May your will be revealed to me concerning my family. In Jesus' name, amen.

Scripture

> Trust in the Lord with all your heart, and lean not on your own understanding; In all your ways acknowledge him, And he shall direct your paths.
>
> Proverbs 3:5-6 (nkjv)

Don't Be Bitter

Pain. Disappointment. Anger. Stress. The combination of these things can make a very bitter woman. Your child's father may have hurt you or even deserted you. What do you do now? If this is your situation, don't worry. You still have a choice. Staying angry is a decision. When someone wrongs you, you decide whether or not, or even how long you will be upset with that person. When you begin to hold a grudge through unforgiveness, bitterness sets in.

Bitterness can be a difficult thing to get out of your heart. Jason and I were young and really didn't understand much about responsibility. Because Jason was still growing in God, I found that my expectations were often disappointed. I learned that a person that is still growing can only give as much as they have.

At that time, I had no understanding of this, so I began to resent him. However, I eventually learned that I had a choice. I knew I didn't want to become an old, hateful woman one day. I knew I shouldn't let anyone's actions, determine how much joy I had on any given day. So, I decided I was tired of being sick and tired. I was tired of feeling down about him and where he was at that point in his life. I decided

I would put all of my hope in Jesus and trust him to bring me through, as well as work on Jason's heart. I believed that one day, Jason would be whole and right where he needed to be.

If you are uncertain or you already know that your child's father will not be in the picture, don't fret. God has already made provision. This does not mean that your child will never have a father figure. God is an awesome God, and he can even change the heart of your child's father. God can send you a godly man. Just pray for his will to be done and be ready to have a walk of patience.

Sometimes, women feel obligated to try to make a relationship work for the sake of the child. It is good to have a working relationship with the child's father, but this is not possible all of the time. Make a decision to put your relationship with your child's father in God's hand. Your Father in heaven knows what's best.

Prayer of Faith

Father, I acknowledge the bitterness and unforgiveness that I have in my heart. I make a decision today to forgive the people that have hurt me. I believe when I forgive others, you forgive me.

Help me to walk in love and freedom. In Jesus' name, amen.

Scriptures

> Be angry, and do not sin. Meditate within your heart on your bed, and be still.
>
> Psalm 4:4 (nkjv)

> But when you are praying, first forgive anyone you are holding a grudge against, so that your Father in heaven will forgive your sins, too.
>
> Mark 11:25 (nlt)

Don't Settle

Nevertheless, if you and your mate manage to maintain a relationship during your pregnancy, be sure you are not settling. The devil always has a counterfeit for God's blessing. God ordained the family to be an institution of love and security. The enemy tries to mimic God's family by using tactics to convince people that living together without the bond of marriage is okay and basically the same thing. Many say, "I don't need a piece of paper to confirm my commitment or love toward my mate." True, a piece of paper does not confirm love. It records that you are legally married. It is not a definition of love.

Why marry then? Marriage is an honorable institution established by God. Marriage is God's idea. Hebrews 13:12 (nkjv) states, "Marriage is honorable among all, and the bed undefiled; but fornicators and adulterers God will judge." The marriage of a man and woman is symbolic of the way Christ loves his church. This cannot be mimicked by a cheap copy of a man and woman playing house. Don't sell yourself short. Doing things God's way is sure to bring more peace and his covering.

If you find yourself in this scenario, pray for God to show you his will for you and your mate. God's way is the only true way of peace. If God is leading you to end the romantic part of your relationship, don't hesitate because of the possible heartache you will have to endure. God knows things you don't know about your mate. You can trust God, even if it means going through a season of heartache. When you are prepared to receive the true mate he has for you, you will see it was well worth going through the pain. The blessing will be that good! Everything will be okay. You can trust God.

Wouldn't you agree that it would be better for you to go through your pregnancy without all the drama? Of course it would. Don't fear being alone. God will be faithful to send you what you need. Just begin to seek him to be your all, and watch how he will comfort you.

The Desire to Be Loved

There are many single women who get pregnant because they want someone to love them. Every woman has a need to be loved, appreciated, and adored. God created us that way. We are his delicate daughters. However, life can sometimes throw such hard blows that many women become tough skinned. Deep down inside, all women have the same need.

Some believe they can receive the love they desire through a mate, but when relationships go bad, all hope may be lost in this area. Children seemingly love unconditionally. When they are very young, mate- rial things don't matter. They would be just as happy playing with a cardboard box and a crayon than the latest electronic toy from the local mega-mart. Even beyond that, they would be happy just to spend time with their parents. It's true love.

More than anything, children require lots of love before they are even born. They receive this love when you take care of yourself during your pregnancy. Exercising, eating right, going for prenatal checkups, praying for your unborn child, and staying away from things that cause you stress are all acts of love for your child.

Put simply, you will do a lot more of giving love to your child than receiving. Of course, they will love you in return, but it will not be what you think you are looking for. The type of love you desire only comes from God. No man, woman, boy, or girl could ever fill that void. Only your heavenly Father can give that type of love. He loves us unconditionally, no matter how many mistakes we have made or how many bad things we have done.

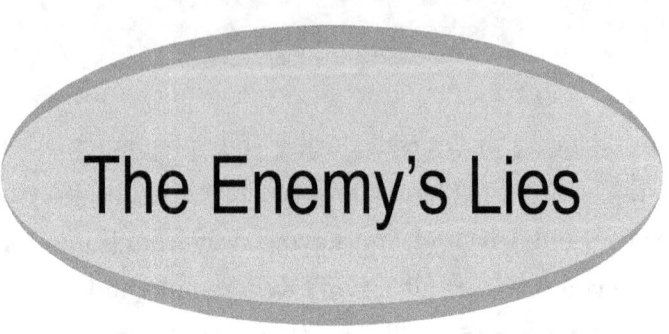

The Enemy's Lies

Let's discuss how the devil can attack. Even after you have fallen to temptation and sin, the devil continues to attack your mind, especially if you did not plan your pregnancy. Understand that the devil directly opposes God's will for your life. He is a liar that desires for God's children to never reach their God-ordained potential. He tries to plant thoughts in your mind that are opposed to God's word. He is the enemy of the saints of God.

Is Pregnancy a Punishment?

John 10:10 (kjv) states: "The thief cometh not, but for to steal, kill, and destroy." The devil, your enemy, will try to steal your destiny, kill your joy, and destroy your hope.

He will do everything he can to keep you from focusing on God's purpose for you and your baby. He will attack your joy by trying to convince you that being pregnant without being married is "punishment" from God.

Friend, allow me to expose this lie from the devil. God hates sin. He is a holy God that requires his children to live holy in order to dwell with him. Fornication (sex before marriage) is a sin, and we as his children must allow God to purify us of any tendencies that we have to fall back into sin.

Our God hates sin, but he loves his creation. This is you, me, and your unborn child. God knows how to hate the sin of a man, but yet love the man. Sometimes man has a problem separating the two, but again, God doesn't.

Being pregnant is not God's way of punishing you. God knows your future. Before you ever made a decision to lie down, God already knew what decision you were going to make. If you walk with him and allow his Spirit to guide your life, he will move you and your child right into your destiny, the place where you were born to be.

Your destiny is a place of fulfillment and purpose. It's the place where the gifts God gave you are put into action. It is a place where he is glorified through your life.

An Accident?

If you did not plan your pregnancy, the devil may also try to convince you that your baby is "an accident." Don't allow the enemy to sow this seed in your mind. If this type of seed began to grow, it would result in thoughts of resentment toward your child. You may even begin to think your child has somehow interrupted your life. This pattern of wrong thinking would only cause further damage by causing you to speak negative things into your child's life. This is why we must fight against the devil's attacks in these areas.

The truth is that there is no such thing as an accidental child to God. God knows the parents of every soul he brings to the earth. This includes the babies that came as a result of rape or incest. God knows and has a purpose for each person. Only God can create a soul. No matter how many times you've had sex without getting pregnant, or if you got pregnant the first time you had sex, God is the one who creates the soul. Just ask a married couple who has been trying for years to have kids without success. Though they may physically be doing everything right, the truth remains, only God can create a soul.

Here's the science of fertilization. During inter-course, a man's ejaculation sends millions of sperm into the vagina. The sperm must make its way through the vagina and into the fallopian tubes. It takes only one sperm to meet and penetrate the outer wall of an egg that is making its monthly trip down the tubes to the uterus. This process is called fertilization. The fertilized egg then rests in the uterus to grow.

Eggs are only ready for fertilization during and right after ovulation. Sperm can live inside you for up to five or even seven days. So, this process must occur perfectly in order for pregnancy to occur as described in scientific terms.

God is the all-knowing. He created the sciences in which we are always discovering new things. He knows when the sperm and egg will meet and a pregnancy will occur. He has already ordained purpose in it all.

Now, let me reiterate some things. By no means am I saying that sex outside of marriage is okay. It is never okay. It is a sin, and God hates sin. However, even in sinful acts of fornication, God is the only creator of life. Remember these things when the enemy tries to attack the purpose of your child.

Get Out of Condemnation

The enemy may attack with lies that your unplanned pregnancy is punishment, or that your baby is an accident. My major attack came through feelings of condemnation. Condemnation is a strong feeling of guilt. It occurs when people have not forgiven themselves for something they have done.

I had a hard time getting past being pregnant. After all, I was supposed to be a "Christian leader." I felt so guilty at times that I didn't want to attend church. I felt as if the self-righteous people were looking down at me. To be honest, some probably were.

I allowed this feeling to continue throughout the duration of my pregnancy. I always wore baggy maternity clothes to help hide my stomach. You may be feeling overwhelmed with the feeling of guilt and shame. Understand this: God will never burden you with condemnation. God convicts, and there is a strong difference.

Condemnation will make you feel down and unfit to be used by God. It is a heavy burden. It does not come from God. God can use anybody for his purposes, especially those who do not have perfect pasts. He is the only one who can give you a fresh start.

Conviction is from God. It will allow you to see the error of your behavior, but encourage you to make better decisions. The Holy Spirit will convict you after you have made a wrong decision, in order to correct you. If you were already a Christian when you became pregnant, you probably felt the conviction of the Holy Spirit before and after having sex. Yielding to the conviction of the Holy Spirit and repenting (making a decision to turn from sinful things) allows us to live the abundant life that Jesus died to give us.

It is always right to follow the leading of the Holy Spirit. As you grow closer to God, you will begin to hear his voice *before* you get into situations that are not profitable for you. I knew that I wasn't in a good situation the night I became pregnant. I knew what being with Jason that night could lead to. But I chose to ignore the leading of God's Spirit, and I fell to the temptation of sexual sin.

Understand that God is sovereign. He already knew what decision I would make that night. He had already made provision. He already knew how he would work out the situation for my good, just as he already knows how he will work things out for you.

For you to avoid the pitfall of condemnation, it is very important for you to renew your mind daily according to Ephesians:

> That you put off, concerning your former conduct, the old man which grows corrupt according to the deceitful lusts, and be renewed in the spirit of your mind, and that you put on the new man which was created according to God, in true righteousness and holiness.
>
> Ephesians 4:22-24 (nkjv)

Today is a new day, and you should no longer think the way you did yesterday. You must be hopeful in God's plan for your life, and the life of your child. God does not condemn you for your past, because he knows that he is powerful enough to cause you to learn and grow from it.

Every time you have a negative thought that would make you feel guilty or unfit to be used of God, you must cast it down. When you ask God to forgive you, he does. He doesn't remember your sin any longer. He will never use it against you, but the enemy will. The devil desires to keep you feeling down, so you will never learn your true purpose, or receive the unfailing love of God. This is why you must make a decision today to forgive yourself and walk in freedom. Oh, the freedom of not having to feel bad! It doesn't make you any more righteous or spiritual to continue to feel condemned after you have genuinely repented to God.

Though the baby is still on the way, know it is not punishment or an accident. God's purpose must be fulfilled in your life and in the life of your child. Let go of condemnation today.

Prayer of Faith

Father, today I give thanks to you for your faithfulness to me. Nothing can separate me from your love. When I sincerely repent to you, you throw my sins as far as the east is from the west. You have purpose for my life, and the life of my child. I let go of any feelings of guilt. Thank you for a fresh start. In your son, Jesus' name, amen.

Scriptures

> Trust in the Lord, and do good; Dwell in the land, and feed on his faithfulness.
>
> Psalms 37:3 (nkjv)

> And I am convinced that nothing can ever separate us from his love. Death can't, and life can't. Our fears for today, our worries about tomorrow, and even the powers of hell can't keep God's love away. Whether we are high above the sky or in the deepest ocean, nothing in all creation will ever be able

to separate us from the love of God that is revealed in Christ Jesus our Lord.

> Romans 8:38-40 (nlt)

As far as the east is from the west, so far has he removed our transgressions from us.

> Psalms 103:12 (niv)

So now there is no condemnation for those who belong to Christ Jesus.

> Romans 8:1 (nlt)

Making the Transition

Now that we have discovered the importance of renewing your mind, it is time to start transitioning for your future as a parent. You are at the dawning of the new day. Things will change, and the perception you have now will determine the outcome of your future.

For example, if you view having a baby as a burden and an unwanted responsibility, think again. It may be true that you would rather not have this responsibility at this point in your life, but this manner of thinking will get you nowhere. Even if you planned your pregnancy, the reality is still that you have a child on the way, and you must make preparations for this transition.

Making Preparations

Making preparations doesn't mean worrying and stressing out. Making preparations means taking things day by day. You might not have it all figured out in one day, one week, or even one month—and that's okay. You will get there. Not understanding this can cause excessive stress. And of course, stress is not good for you or your baby. Not knowing simple things like how you will buy maternity clothes can send any pregnant women with financial struggles on an emotional roller coaster.

This is why during this transition you must learn how to put your trust in God. You may not know all the answers, or be sure about the questions that you should be asking, but God knows what he has prepared for you each day. Already, your way has been made. God already knows who will be your child's babysitter and where your child's daycare will be. To be able to rest knowing these things are already taken care of takes faith in God.

When we believe God to take care of us, it pleases him. During your pregnancy, pray about everything. Pray about which doctor to choose. Pray during each doctor visit. Pray and also praise. When we praise God by thanking him for the things we ask him to do before we see them done, it is an act of faith. Begin praising God now for the provision you will see him bring. Even praise God when you are uncertain about your future. When you do this, it shows God that you are depending on him.

Life Adjustments

It was the end of the semester during my second year in college when I discovered that I was pregnant. After much thought, I decided it would be best for me to take night classes for the remainder of the year and work full time during the day. This was different for me, but it was important for me to remain in school.

I tried it. My job was great, but working eight hours a day and acting as a full-time student at night proved to be too much for me. Consequently, I withdrew from the university during the middle of the semester and continued to work full-time, even though this decision had consequences. Withdrawing in the middle of the semester caused me to lose my scholarship that paid most of my tuition. Nevertheless, this was an adjustment that I had to make. It was my desire to finish college, and though I wasn't sure how, I knew eventually I would finish. So, I continued to work for a local IT corporation in our city as an administrative assistant.

Things were not easy at home. Before I found out I was pregnant, I shared an apartment with my cousin who also attended the same university. Sure, living on my own at nineteen was fun and free, but I soon discovered how hard it was to pay bills monthly on part-time income while trying to study and maintain a decent GPA. So, in an effort to save money and focus more on my studies, I decided to move back home with my mother who lived alone in the outskirts of the city.

For me, it wasn't easy adjusting to doing things my mother's way after becoming so accustomed to doing whatever, whenever I wanted. We clashed. We argued. We even had days where we stopped speaking. She had problems with the way I kept the house. I had a problem with the temperature she liked the thermostat to stay on.

It didn't matter how big or how small the issue. We always found ourselves at odds. Then, the bombshell hit.

I was pregnant. How would she handle such news when we already had a strain in our relationship?

I waited about three weeks to tell her the news. She was very upset. So upset that she just left the house. I knew she was hurt and disappointed. In my emotions, I made a decision to move. *Bad idea.* As I mentioned before, this was not the time to make a permanent decision, but at the time, I didn't know that. All I knew was that I didn't want to have to live in the face of her disappointment.

After she had some time to take everything in, I shared with her my desire to move. She didn't necessarily agree with my decision, but she supported my decision. We even went looking for apartments together. After a few weeks, I decided I would move into a one-bedroom apartment. It wasn't the most luxurious place in the world, but it would do. I paid rent at that apartment for about three months, then I moved back home with my mother. Can you imagine the money I wasted for just three months?

I would like to take this moment to remind you to do your best not to make emotional decisions. These decisions are usually based in fear or pride. The temptation to make an emotional decision will be strong, but you still have the option to choose wisdom. The wisest choice may not be what is really comfortable for you, but you can trust God to help you through it. Pray before you make decisions, whether big or small. Ask God to lead you and help you. He is always faithful to do so.

What's the Real Motivation?

I felt having my own place before the baby was born would be best. Now, I understand the *real* reason I moved out was because of pride and selfishness. I wanted to prove to anyone that tried to look down on me that I was going to make it, and I didn't need anyone's help. However, that didn't last very long. Though I was working full time, I didn't make much money, which made staying on my own a strain. I was ignoring the provision that God had already provided for me by being at home with my mother.

Don't let pride make you miss the provision that God has for you in this season. Before you make any major decisions, think about the *real* reason you are making them. What's your motivation? Is it pride? Are you making the best decision for you *and* your baby? Are you being selfish? I could have saved all the money

I wasted moving out trying to prove a point. God will use many people in this season to help you with whatever need you have, whether it is financial or not. Gratefully accept whatever provision God is providing for you right now. You will have more peace in your life if you receive what he is providing for you, rather than making things harder on yourself by doing it your way.

Know That God Has Heard

At times, it may seem as though God has not heard your prayers. You may feel God is not concerned about your concerns. These feelings are far from the truth. I remember having the same feelings while I was sitting alone in my bedroom. I wondered if God would be able to get me out of the mess I had made. It was around that time when

I came to the realization that Jason would not be there for me during the pregnancy. I began to see him as being immature. I thought, *I never dreamed the family I have always wanted would start like this.*

In the midst of my pity party, Miyake (my best friend who had recently moved five hundred miles away) called me on the phone. She said, "I have a word from God for you. He told me to tell you that he has heard, and he will deliver." What a word! She had no idea about how I was wondering whether God could get me out of the mess I had made. I was so encouraged. I held on to this word for the duration of my pregnancy. I began believing God heard my prayers. I began believing that he would deliver me from failure, poverty, doubt, and anything else that would come against the purpose that he had for me.

It was during the last trimester of my pregnancy that Miyake's words really came alive. I was discussing possible baby names with a coworker and friend named Kristi. I told her that I was thinking of the name "Javen," which was a name Jason suggested during my few conversations with him. I wasn't completely sold on the name when

Kristi excitingly blurted, "How about Jaiden?" Immediately, I loved it. Names with meanings were important to me, so I decided to research its meaning. I discovered that "Jaiden" meant, "God has heard." I was instantly sold. I knew this was the name for my daughter.

Today, my daughter's name is a constant reminder that God hears my prayers, and he does deliver. Your deliverance will manifest as well. Endure the trying times. Always pray knowing God hears your prayers, and all things will work together for your good, because you love God.

Day by Day and Hour by Hour

I will be honest, it was not easy. Some people decide to take things one day at a time. I couldn't make it that long. I was so overwhelmed some days that I had to take it hour by hour. I had to renew my mind with scriptures about joy. Otherwise, my heart would be filled with depression and anger.

I would start my day by saying, "No matter what comes my way for the next few hours, I am making the decision to be happy no matter what." During that time, I would meditate on scriptures about joy. Before long, I could make it through the day and even have a smile on my face.

God's word is powerful enough to overcome any negative emotion in your life. His word is life and peace. Meditate on God's word more than you worry about your tomorrow. His word is more than enough to provide you with peace today. Make a decision not to become bitter. Your life will be much more enjoyable when you set all of your hope in the Lord.

Below are some scriptures about joy. Meditate on these. Memorize them. Quote them all day long. Believe them, and watch joy come alive in your life.

Prayer of Faith

Father, you are my joy and my strength. It is not your desire for me to be down. Help me to walk by faith in your word and not by what I see happening in my life today. I believe that you are working everything out for me. I believe you are equipping me with everything I need to be a good parent. Thank you for your blessings. In Jesus' name, amen.

Scriptures

> Do not sorrow, for the joy of the Lord is your strength.
>
> Nehemiah 8:10 (nkjv)

> For we walk by faith, not by sight.
>
> 2 Corinthians 5:7 (nkjv)

> Every scripture is God-breathed (given by his inspiration) and profitable for instruction, for reproof and conviction of sin, for correction of error and discipline in obedience, [and] for training in righteousness (in holy living, in conformity to God's will in thought, purpose, and action), so that the man of God may be complete and proficient, well fitted and thoroughly equipped for every good work.
>
> 2 Timothy 3:16-18 (amp)

Promotion

It may take some time, and it will definitely take endurance, but if you put God first in *all* things, he will bring you out on top every time. It's a new beginning. Start now with your new way of thinking. Your best days are ahead of you. You have a new journey of discovering God's purpose for you and your child.

I must tell you that everything will not be revealed to you at once, and even this is an act of God's love! If he showed you everything good he has planned for your life now, you probably wouldn't believe him! God will reveal it to you in his time, and you can trust that as long as you remain in him, things will get better.

Jeremiah 29:11 (nkjv) state, "For I know the thoughts that I think toward you, says the Lord, thoughts of peace and not evil, to give you a future and a hope." This is your promotion, becoming a parent. A new day to step up to a fresh start. Imagine the great purpose that the Lord has for his special creation that is growing inside of you right now. Imagine how the Lord will lead you as a parent to impart great things into this child as only you can! What a hope and a future! The possibilities are limitless, but God already knows. According to Psalm 127:3 (nlt), "Children are a gift from the Lord, they are a reward from him." You are chosen by God to bring forth greatest into the earth. Stay connected to God through your prayer time with him, and allow him to reveal the plans he has already made for you and your child's destiny.

Don't Give Up on Your Destiny

One does not reach her destiny overnight. There may be some hard days on the road to your destiny, but God will be faithful to be with you through them all. God knew that you would conceive a child on the journey to your destiny. He has already made provision and ordained purpose in it all. What a mighty God we serve! Our God can take the messes and mistakes we make and cause them all to work out for our good. Romans 8:28 (nkjv) reads, "And we know that all things work together for good to them that love God, to them who are the called according to his purpose."

When you love God and genuinely have a heart to serve him, you are not disqualified when you make a mistake. When we sincerely repent to God, he forgives us. Though you may not be able to see how all of this will work out right now, know that through God, it will. Through the process of time, you will see how he will restore everything you lost. You will see how he will restore your joy for all the tears you cried.

Miscarriages

Miscarriages are a reality in this world. They come with much pain and suffering. It's a very real concern most women contemplate at some point during their pregnancy. Statistically speaking, it is a fact someone who reads this book may have this experience. I want to let you know that, even in these heartfelt tragedies, God is still in control and still has purpose. I want to encourage you to stay close to God and seek him for comfort and peace.

It is always the enemy's plan to use pain to move you away from God. However, it is always God's plan to use the pain and things we do not understand to draw us closer to him.

One thing I can say with assurance is that God is a God of comfort and purpose. Don't go through your pregnancy fearing the worst for yourself. Fear of the future paralyzes you and keeps you from enjoying your present state. Give each day over to God and have peace knowing God rules in sovereignty and love. Not one child is ever lost to him.

Prayer of Faith

Father, I acknowledge you as the only sovereign God. I put all my trust in you. I will not fear. Let your purposes come to pass in my life. In Jesus' name, amen.

Scriptures

I knew you before I formed you in your mother's womb ...

Jeremiah 1:5 (nlt)

Jesus said, "Let the little children come to me, and do not hinder them, for the kingdom of heaven belongs to such as these."

Matthew 19:14 (niv)

It's All about Seeds

When a flower seed has been planted in good soil, there is a waiting period. The type of seed determines how short or long the waiting period is. When the seed receives adequate sunlight and water for nourishment, it begins to grow. The stem forms and the petals grow. Soon, a beautiful flower is developed. The same is true of a child. It starts as a very tiny embryo that grows into a fetus, and in nine months, a baby.

The same is also true of the word of God. We become "impregnated" with the seed, which is God's word. In a period of time, that seed begins to grow in us as it is "watered" or "nourished" by our faith and the words we speak. Eventually, through the process of time, we begin to see what was originally a seed, or a word from God (whether spoken to you personally or by reading scriptures from the Bible), manifest in our lives.

Let me explain further. When you pray and seek God's will during your pregnancy, he will reveal his future plans for your life. This is what I am referring to as "seed" or "word" from God. God may tell you that you are going to be richly blessed. He may tell you that you will have financial prosperity while you have no money in the bank. You may not see how what God said is ever going to come to pass. This is where your faith comes into action. It's *believing* what God said, no matter what. Hebrews 11:1 (nkjv) reads, "Faith is the substance of things hoped for, the evidence of things not seen." It's what you hope for, but you see no signs of it yet. Faith is believing in God. It's believing that he will see you through, no matter what comes against you. God is not a liar. You will see your destiny manifest if you don't give up on your faith in God.

Seeds to Sow

When a farmer plants seeds in a field, in time, he expects to see his harvest. He plants with expectation. The same must be true for you as it relates to your finances. A lot of times, being a single parent can be a financial strain. This is why you must plant seeds expecting a harvest.

For example, when a farmer plants his seeds, he doesn't just plant them anywhere on any piece of land. He specifically places the seeds in land that has been tilled and is fertile (good ground that is capable of producing). When you give your money (seed planting) and consistently give your tithe (ten percent of all your income) to your local church, you open the door for God's blessing. Malachi states:

> "Bring all the tithes into the storehouse, that there may be food in My house, and try me now in this," says the Lord of hosts, "If I will not open for you the windows of heaven and pour out for you such blessing that there will not be room enough to receive it."
>
> Malachi 3:10 (nkjv)

Giving your money to God is a form of submission and honor to him. You shouldn't give out of obligation and still expect to receive the blessings mentioned in Malachi, but you should give out of love because it honors him and advances his kingdom on the earth.

It takes faith to sow seeds of money. This is a biblical principle that will open doors for you to receive even more of God's blessing over your finances. Yes, it is true that there are many rich people who do not tithe or give to advance the kingdom of God. However, they may be rich, but their prosperity is not covered by the hand of God. Malachi 3:11 (nkjv) states that God will "rebuke the devourer for our sakes." That means, when the devil tries to attack, God will step in and rebuke the enemy! Remember, we give because we love and honor God, not out of obligation. It is from *this* type of giving that we can expect a harvest.

Sown in Faith

While I was living in my apartment during my pregnancy, I often watched a famous televangelist named Rod

Parsley. The Holy Spirit spoke to me during the broadcast to sow ten dollars to help the ministry and aid some people in need.

I was already financially strained, so sowing ten dollars was not appealing to me at all. I decided that God wasn't talking to me and tried to ignore the tugging of the Holy Spirit. When I realized playing dumb wasn't fooling God, I thought, *Okay, God, I heard you. You know I don't have much money, and what is ten dollars going to help anyway?* In that instant, the televangelist said, "If you sow ten dollars, we will match it." *Okay, God, I will do it,* I thought.

I knew God was calling me to take a step of faith in my finances. I knew he wanted me to trust him. God was not trying to take something from me. He was simply providing himself a way to get something to me. There are principles in the word of God. In God's kingdom, you give then you receive your increase based on your heart in giving. God was setting me up. At the time, I didn't know God was going to use the financial seed I sowed to bring about a much-needed harvest.

During the end of my eighth month of pregnancy, I began to have contractions. My water broke, and my doctor had no choice but to prepare for the delivery of a baby that was coming a month early. I hadn't planned to be off from work until a month later. What would I do about bills? What about the four weeks of pay that I wouldn't get because the baby was coming early? God wasn't worried. He had already made a way.

After the successful delivery of healthy, beautiful, baby girl, I returned home. A week later, I received a check in the mail for the previous two weeks that I had worked. However, with this check, I unexpectedly received *hundreds of dollars* from my coworkers! Since they weren't able to throw me the surprise baby shower they were planning, they decided to take up cash instead! On top of that, I was paid an extra week's pay! I just began to cry. I was amazed at how God took my ten dollar seed and multiplied it by the hundreds. Though I didn't actually sow a very big seed, it was a *very big* sacrifice to me at the time, which required a lot of my faith, and God honored it.

God wants to do the same thing and more with your finances. Allow him to provide you with opportunities to give. Remember, when you give with a pure heart of faith and following the leading of his spirit, you are making an investment in yourself and your baby's future.

Prayer of Faith

Father, I am making a decision to trust you with my finances. Help me to be obedient to you with my money. I believe I will reap a harvest from the seeds that I sow. In Jesus' name, amen.

Scriptures

> For whoever desires to save his life will lose it, but whoever loses his life for My sake will find it. For what profit is it to a man if he gains the whole world, and loses his own soul? Or what will a man give in exchange for his soul?
>
> Matthew 16:25 (nkjv)

SINGLE AND PREGNANT

I assure you that you can say to this mountain, May God lift you up and throw you into the sea,' and your command will be obeyed. All that's required is that you really believe and do not doubt in your heart. You can pray for anything, and if you believe, you will have it. But when you are praying, first forgive anyone you are holding a grudge against, so that your Father in heaven will forgive your sins, too.

Matthew 11:23-25 (nlt)

But this I say: he who sows sparingly will also reap sparingly, and he who sows bountifully will also reap bountifully.

2 Corinthians 9:6 (nkjv)

Manifested Victory

I don't know many women who desire to be single their entire lives. Most women have always dreamed of having a family since childhood. Even though your family may not start as picture perfect as you had intended, don't give up on your dream. Having a less- than-perfect past does not determine your future.

I always wanted a family. I was raised in a single parent home. I was my mother's only child, so the idea of family fascinated me. When I got pregnant, the devil told me I would never have my desire. In spite of this lie from the devil, God led me to the truth in his word. This scripture would become the foundation of my faith in believing that one day I would still have my family.

> Do not throw away this confident trust in the Lord, no matter what happens. Remember the great reward it brings you! Patient endurance is what you need now, so you will continue to do God's will. Then you will receive all that he has promised.
>
> Hebrews 10:36-38 (nlt)

I knew that I would have to wait a while and endure some things. But I stand now in complete victory as an overcomer. I made it through the hard times of my pregnancy. I finished college (though it took a little longer) and graduate school. I bought a brand-new home at age twenty-four. My daughter and I are very happy. I am not bitter or prideful.

Most importantly, God fixed the situation that could not be fixed. He healed my heart and made me whole. I do not resent my child's father. I prayed and I have faith that one day, God would transform him as well. That day has begun. Over a period of years, God has been working on his heart. Jason has begun to put forth effort in developing a good relationship with his daughter. He has even expressed the desire to be the best father that he can be, and I believe he will be just that. This is the result of much prayer and faith, and it can happen for you too. God is not finished yet. We take things day by day, trusting God.

I know now, all things are possible through Christ, no matter what statistics say. Yet, this is not the end of my story. I am still believing God for the manifestation of the family that I have always wanted. I am very confident that in his time, God will fulfill this desire as well.

Free to a New Beginning

God will drop things in your spirit when you have a heart to allow him to be your peace and joy. I realized my relationship with Jason was not going to work. It was a very hard to accept this initially. In an effort to avoid falling into discouragement, I began to pray and cry out to my Father. I am so glad God hears and answers prayers. That day, God answered me with a poem. Though I am not a poet, these simple words encouraged me that day and many days afterwards. It gave me hope and excitement for the new day I was entering. I want to leave you with this poem. I hope it will serve as encouragement for you to leave the pain and past mistakes behind. Look forward to your glorious and purposeful future. May God continue to bless you as you walk into your new beginning.

Free to a New Beginning

Oh yes, oh yes
I am finally free

Free to a new beginning
Free to a whole new me

Oh yes, I am free from bondage
and free from sin
But oh no, I can never go back
to that kind of pain again

You see, I'm free now,
yes, free at last

I'm starting something new and
throwing away the past

Oh yes, I'm free, free at last, free indeed
Life with Jesus Christ,

That's how I'll succeed.
                                    -Sharllette Berry

God sets the solitary in families ...
                                    Psalms 68:6 (nkjv)

Living the Promise

It gives me great joy to write this bonus chapter for you. I felt it was very important to let you know the end of the matter. God's promises are always sure. Today, as I write this, I am celebrating ten years of marriage! That's right. God fulfilled His promise to me, and I have been married for 10 years! Not only did he bless me with a wonderful husband, he blessed me with three more children! My husband had two boys and a girl from a previous marriage. Together, we have four children! Later, God gave us the surprise blessing of a girl of our own! Can you imagine that, a family of 7?! I would call that a double portion!

My family is the most important thing to me on this earth. In ten years, we have certainly had our challenges and had situations that caused us to grow. Family has made life so sweet, and the good days by far outweigh the bad days.

I still remember the road to obtaining my promise. It was certainly a walk of faith, and many of those days my faith fell very short. But that didn't stop God. If God promises it, you can take it to the bank. Yes, if you want it, a family is for you. Keep believing. Rest in it while you believe. Don't be consumed with it. God knows how to fit the pieces of your puzzle together. He has a plan. Don't waste your days in sorrow wishing that the promise would hurry and come to pass. Be faithful with the things that he has put in your heart today, and that alone will be plenty to keep you busy. Have the right focus and stay the course. Enjoy each day and at the right time, your promise will manifest. Blessings to you and yours, and your beautiful future.

-Sharllette

www.ingramcontent.com/pod-product-compliance
Lightning Source LLC
Chambersburg PA
CBHW062142100526
44589CB00014B/1668